INTO THE DARKNESS

HOOK YOUR READERS (WITHOUT GETTING LOST IN THE DARK)

DAVID WRIGHT

For the misfits

FOREWORD

Dave is a dark guy.

Probably the darkest I know.

Okay, for sure the darkest I know. Maybe by an order of magnitude.

I don't want to spoil anything for you, so I'lll let him tell you the Dead Baby on Christmas story. Those words alone should give you a glimpse into the messiness you're about to read.

But I also have some great news — it isn't all doom and gloom because despite Dave's reputation, that isn't the kind of writer he is. I wouldn't be able to write with him if it was.

Dave is thoughtful and explores the crevices of insanity in an effort to protect his own psyche. He finds solace in those hollows, knowing he can use

the cracks and fissures to help inoculate himself
from the world's unending horrors.

He sees them everywhere, which makes sense
since he never stops looking. We're opposite in
this way. Dave thinks I bury my head in the sand.
I don't, though I do admit to doing only a barely
reasonable job of keeping up with the news.
That's because I understand what it is and that
consumption has a downside. The news causes us
stress, anxiety, and fatigue due in part to the way
it affects our sleep. And it's habit forming; the
more you get, the more you want. Yes, it's important to stay informed, but it's those publications'
job to whip you into a needless frenzy. They're
drawing from the dregs of humanity because
those stories are the outliers rather than the norm.
That's what makes them worthy of being on the
news.

Dave and I are wired differently in this way. And
in many, many others.

But that's great for all of us.

I'm lucky to write with Dave. I appreciate that
he's willing to go places I never would if I were
writing alone. Our collaboration lends my work a
darkness and depth it wouldn't otherwise possess.
Dave's drafts often force me to confront situations I

would normally turn away from. He doesn't have boundaries like my other partner, Johnny.

Nothing is off limits with Dave, but Johnny has rules. Nothing can happen to children or animals. I've inserted both types of events into outlines that Johnny didn't write because he understands his limits. But for Dave, those fences are part of the art itself, and I become his co-conspirator.

Navigating these dark scenarios is usually much more fun with Dave than it should be, but that's because everything is always handled with an intelligence and longing to understand. Dave hates "torture porn" or unnecessary violence. He's a much softer man than most people realize, and his fascination with humanity's underbelly comes from a place of fear rather than anything even remotely resembling admiration.

I've pushed Dave in a lot of ways. He's long said if I hadn't pushed him into publishing his first book, it never would have happened. But Dave has pushed me, too. He's encouraged me to grow as a writer by delving into the darkness alongside him.

There are many things he can do that I cannot.

Which is why it was so important that he write this book.

By the time you're done reading this, you will

understand how to tap into your own darkness to tell a better story, grow as a storyteller, and deeply engage your readers in ways you never have before. You will know how to write a better book using the fears and beliefs that are fueling many of your ideas and actions already.

Dave has written and published millions of words and connected with readers all over the world. He's been right there in the wings as Johnny and I have built out our studio and worked with dozens of storytellers to grow ourselves and the industry. But it's his perspective that provides the most value because you never know where it might take you.

I wanted Dave to write this book for you because I know better than anyone else in the world exactly how much he has to offer.

For the longest time, he refused to write nonfiction because he didn't believe he had anything worthy to say and wanted to leave such things to me and Johnny.

But what Dave has a difficult time realizing is that while some storytellers might cheer along with the things Johnny and I are doing, many more can identify with his struggles.

He finally saw it. Then he agreed to write this book for me and you.

As always, I love his work, but this one has left me feeling more grateful than usual. Dave wrote something vulnerable that is bound to change you if you let it.

Please read it, review it, and encourage our Dave to write more.

Sean Platt

August 2019

INTRODUCTION

I like dark stories.

But not for the reasons most people might assume.

I believe there's a misconception about horror and other dark tales, particularly among people who don't read or watch the genre. They seem to think if you're into horror, you must enjoy watching people in fear and pain.

When meeting new people, I'm often nervous to tell them what I really write.

I write lots of stuff — horror, sci-fi, thrillers, and dark or urban fantasy. But saying I write all that feels like I'm rambling. It's easiest to just tell them I write horror.

They either nod in approval or look at me like I

just told them I dismember bodies in my dungeon basement on the weekends.

Pro tip: Never dismember bodies on the weekends. Too many people around. Wait for a time when neighbors are less likely to walk by and hear the bone saw.

"Oh ..." they say. "Horror is too dark for me."

Or they ask why I'd want to write about such ugly things. It's almost like they want to ask the question my wife often asks when I tell her about some disturbing new story idea. "What is wrong with you?" As if I revel in the horrors, taking pleasure in writing the darkest things I can imagine.

Actually, I do take pleasure in coming up with something so clever or twisted that it'll scare the hell out of people. But that's not quite the same as enjoying the subject matter like some murder aficionado at home with my collection of serial killer trading cards.

Oooh, I'll trade you two John Wayne Gacy's for a rookie season Ted Bundy.

A lot of times people will say something like, "With so many horrors in the real world, I don't need them in my books, TV, or movies as well. It's just too much."

And I get it.

I really get it. The world is a shit show. I'm not sure if it's any more of a shit show than it's always been. We're just so connected now to the news, to social media, and to others, that we're hyper aware of all the festering shit all day every day. And ... it can be overwhelming.

I feel the same away about the more brutal horror movies that play out like the fantasies of a snuff film fetishist or movies that are so unrelentingly nihilistic they leave you feeling empty after you've watched them. I wouldn't want more of that in my life.

I don't like those kinds of dark stories. I'm not judging, you sick bastard. But they don't do much for me. They're too bleak, and I hate feeling utterly hopeless after I finish a book or watch a movie.

And that's probably how most people feel about any horror or dark story.

So, yeah, I get it.

Yet, I love the horror genre. I love dark fiction, in books, television, and film. Some of my favorite shows are fairly dark — *Breaking Bad*, *The Wire*, and *The Walking Dead*. But I don't enjoy these shows because of all the horrible things that happen in them. I like them for a different reason.

I enjoy dark narratives because the world is a dark place.

And because I want to believe there's a light at the end of the tunnel — one that preferably isn't a train headed straight at me.

I like dark stories because they help me better understand the darkness in the world and sometimes even cope with it.

I like dark stories because they offer catharsis and hope that despite all the shit going on in the world today, you can't turn away from the light. Even in the darkest and coldest of nights, there is always at least a glimmer of hope.

And maybe these fictional stories are an illusion, a bedtime story to convince you you'll be okay. But sometimes we need an illusion because it's the only thing that makes us able to brave the darkness.

HEY, DAVE. WANNA WRITE A BOOK?

When my writing partner, Sean Platt, approached me about writing this book, my first instinct was to say no.

That's almost always my first instinct when it comes to non-fiction, especially books about writing — which I've more or less avoided while Sean and his other writing partner, Johnny B.

Truant, have written several excellent titles on craft.

Despite having been a co-host on The Self-Publishing Podcast and The Story Studio Podcast, I've never felt particularly comfortable talking about story at length.

Despite my success with series like *Yesterday's Gone*, and smaller successes with *No Justice*, *White-Space*, and having sold one movie script to date, I can't help but compare myself to the biggest stars of the genre — Stephen King, Dean Koontz, and other household names.

What do I have to say that those huge authors can't say better?

And Sean gave me an answer that changed my mind.

"You have your story, Dave. Your process. They can't talk about your story or your process."

I thought about me as a kid and as a teen, about how desperate I was for something that would've helped me figure out what to do with all the darkness inside me. Then I thought about how to channel it into fiction.

I would've loved a book like this. A book that told me it wasn't just okay to write about dark things, but it might very well be necessary for my well-being to record these thoughts, to explore what they mean to me and to the world.

And that's why I agreed to write *Into the Darkness*.

This isn't a book full of rules on How You Should Write Your Book.

First off, I don't even know all the rules to writing, at least not in any instructional sort of way. I know just enough to get by on most days. But for the most part, I'm learning as I go, forever a student of the books, TV, and movies I love.

But there are no rules on writing set in stone. Not really, if you think about it. Yeah, there are grammar rules and things you should definitely learn if you want to make a career of this. But ... they aren't rules so much as accepted standards. For every rule identified by an expert, you can easily find someone else who did the exact opposite and somehow managed to create a kick-ass story.

This isn't a book of rules.

It's a book about how I understand darkness and its place in story.

About how I like to do things, explaining some of my story choices and how I make dark fiction that people enjoy reading.

But if you have a way that works, or if my advice or writing doesn't click for you, that's cool.

You do you.

So who is this book for?

Glad you asked, reader in the future somehow asking me questions.

This is a book for the lonely teenage me sitting in the back of the class scribbling stories for escape from bullies.

This is a book for those of you who struggle with the darkness, both in the world and within yourself.

This is a book for our readers who might be curious to learn a bit more about our process and how we feel our way through the stories we tell.

This is a book, that at its heart, isn't just about the dark, but also the light. And in our darkest times, it's more important than ever that we hold onto the light.

But first, we must be willing to explore the darkness.

1

MY DARK ORIGIN STORY

I USED TO LIKE PEOPLE.

When I was a child in the seventies and eighties, I saw the world through different eyes. People were generally nice, parents were firm but loving, strangers weren't yet a danger, and if you worked hard enough, you could be anything you wanted to be. I was like a happy puppy, always expecting a smiley face.

Then, when I was in grade school, I watched my mother get mugged in front of me.

We were riding a bike, me in the child's seat on the rear, to Winn-Dixie for some groceries while my father was at work. We'd just come out of the store and she was about to put me on the back of the bike when a guy ran up to us with a gun demanding she hand over her purse.

It was the first moment in my life when I realized you can be a good person, do all the right things, spend years raising a child, then another person could fuck that all up in one violent moment.

Fortunately, the guy took her purse and didn't hurt my mother. Otherwise, this would be Batman's origin story, not mine.

Well, my parents weren't rich, so it would've been more like Blue Collar Batman's origin story.

Note to self: Write that story!

While it didn't end in tragedy, it was scary as hell for my mother and me. And not just in that moment. When you're a victim of a violent crime, that tends to have more than a few lingering effects. You're nervous around people you don't know. You're skittish. You have flashbacks. And that's just a few of the longstanding effects.

I remember staring helplessly, for the first time realizing that the world wasn't the innocent place of wonder that I'd read about in kid's stories until that point. It was a scary place, and sometimes bad things happened to good people for no good reason.

Our once peaceful neighborhood that seemed like something out of a 1950's era TV show was changing and quickly becoming a violent place. The sort of place where drugs, gangs, and poverty spread like cancer until all hope was choked out and the world I knew became hard to recognize.

In the few years that followed:

- a man tried to drag me into the bushes at knifepoint, only to be chased away by a neighbor.
- a carload of assholes chased me down on Halloween night wanting to hurt me.
- a man peeked into my bathroom window while I was on the toilet.
- I walked outside my back door to find a man crawling through the window of my neighbor's house behind me.
- and one afternoon while my parents were gone, I was sitting in the living room watching TV when I looked over to see a shadow fall over our frosted jalousie windows on the front door. Moments later, a man's hand began to pull the windows out in order to reach in and unlock my door. I ran out the back terrified, trying to put as much distance

between the intruder and myself that I could.

And a part of me never stopped running.

Despite all of those close calls with violence, and more that I'm leaving out for brevity's sake, I was one of the lucky ones.

I wasn't the victim of a drive-by shooting, though I had guns pulled on me. I wasn't successfully kidnapped (and whatever else that man wanted to do to me). And my family managed to get out of the neighborhood before it swallowed us whole.

And I still had an incredibly lucky childhood compared to sooooo many other kids in the world who are born into abject poverty, slavery, and/or abusive situations they can't ever escape. That's to say nothing of children who don't even get a shot at life before disease or starvation takes them. The fact that I was fortunate enough to be born in America at a time of peace and relative economic stability is not lost on me. So I feel a bit weird talking about a few scary situations and bullying when there are far more serious problems out there.

But in order to understand why I write the things I do or am the person I am, I must return to the formative years that woke me to this world's darkness.

If that man who mugged my mother was my first glimpse of evil, then the TV miniseries *Roots* ripped off the blinders the rest of the way. The show's exploration of slavery was the first time I saw evil perpetrated on a larger scale — and even sanctioned by society. I couldn't fathom how anybody could justify owning and abusing other people for any reason. It was mind-blowing and deeply unsettling.

If mankind was capable of that, what else was it willing to do?

I had not yet learned of the Holocaust, the Nanking Massacre, the Thirty Years' War, the Inquisition, or any of the other atrocities man has perpetrated on one another all throughout history.

When *Roots* aired on TV, I was one of the only white kids on my block. Despite this being the 1970s and racial tensions being played out on TV and in the news, it wasn't something I'd given much thought to since most of my friends were black. We always got along fine, and their parents were nice to me.

I was blissfully ignorant of so much of this country's racist history and had no idea people were being treated differently because of their skin color.

Roots was an atom bomb on my ignorance.

The show made me aware of slavery. I can't remember if we'd yet learned about it in first grade, but I don't think so. Even if I had heard of it somewhere, television has a way of putting a human face on suffering and history that makes it feel real. Seeing slaves tortured onscreen horrified and confused me.

How could people do this to each other?

But *Roots* also made me aware of just how different I was from my neighbors.

It wasn't a problem to me. But unfortunately, it became a problem to some of them, including the older brother of one of my good friends.

I went over to this kid's house all the time, and I loved his family. His older brother taught me to play checkers. We'd play ball in their yard and on the streets until it got dark outside.

After *Roots*, my friend's older brother suddenly hated me, calling me a cracker and white devil. He accused me of calling him "the N-word."

I hadn't, of course.

But he wanted to kick my ass.

He chased me down the street.

Somehow, I outran him. I don't know if my friend or his other siblings had stopped his brother from catching up to me or what. I only remember hiding in bushes, crying and confused, not knowing what the hell was going on.

Suddenly, overnight, everything had changed.

And I couldn't tell my parents what happened.

It would become this big thing, and I didn't know where it would go from there. Maybe they wouldn't let me be friends with any black kids — assuming any of my old friends even wanted to be friends anymore.

It was a confusing time, and I wanted to know why people suddenly hated me. I certainly hadn't done anything. Nor had I changed from the kid they once knew.

I decided to do a bit of reading about slavery and other horrible things men have done to one another throughout our millennia on this planet.

I became quickly obsessed with a different question: what caused people to hurt each other?

Not only that, but how could evil occur on such a massive scale? It required a level of hate I couldn't fathom, but something else, as well. Because what else could possibly explain why decent people would ignore such horrors as slavery, the Holocaust, and (truly) countless others?

What turned otherwise seemingly normal people into monsters?

And if those people could become unwitting barbarians, what about the rest of us? What thin lines separate us from those who commit or turn a blind eye to atrocities? And what, if anything, could we do to stop it?

Those questions still puzzle me today.

I still can't understand the shit people do. Babies aren't programmed for evil. You don't see toddlers trying to kill each other. What is it that turns people into monsters?

Unfortunately, there isn't an easy answer or simple solution.

Evil acts can be the result of traumatic events, psychological disorders, socioeconomic and political alienation, manipulation, and a host of other reasons.

Or, as my father would say, shit just sometimes happens.

As the neighborhood got worse and crime around us escalated, my father decided it was time to move our family out to the suburbs. We couldn't afford it. But he sacrificed, busting his ass working construction to keep us all safe.

It was a good place to grow up. Violent crime

hadn't yet moved to the suburbs, and we were more insulated than we had been before. It was almost like being back in that innocent bubble I'd been in before things went bad.

But one thing hadn't changed.

I was still different.

Now I wasn't the white kid. I was the poor kid. The socially awkward, painfully shy, and very naive kid. And soon, the fat zit-faced kid. I was the kid with Obsessive Compulsive Disorder who would blink, walk backward through doors, repeat himself, constantly count things, and all the other weird shit I did.

Back then, OCD wasn't really understood. I didn't even know I had it, let alone have any sort of identifying name to help understand what might be wrong with me. Other kids just thought I was a twitchy, blinky freak.

And when you're different as a kid, for any reason, the majority has a way of crushing you.

In my first few days there, this kid, whom we'll call Tony, befriended me. We were in fifth grade, but he was already strong and worked out all the time. And he was really cool and popular.

He invited me to hang out with him at his house. I was surprised by how quickly I'd not only made a friend, but a popular one! Maybe I wouldn't stick out here. Maybe I would fit right in.

I went over to his house.

He said I should lift weights with him. I wasn't yet fat, but I wasn't athletic, either.

I said okay, though I didn't know how to do it. He said he'd show me. He told me to lift a barbell over my head while standing up.

I did it, and he acted impressed.

He had a dumbbell in his hand. And he was looking at me with this glee in his eyes that I had never seen before. I thought he was thinking of a funny joke, something he was about to tell me.

Turns out, I was the joke.

He took that barbell and hit me straight in the balls.

It was brutal. And he was laughing like a maniac before calling me a "pussy ass faggot" and telling me to get out of his house.

I didn't understand it.

I walked home crying. I went home and told my mother who did the absolute worst thing she could do. She went to his house and yelled at him. And he then insulted her, in front of pretty much every kid in the neighborhood.

It was humiliating. And it set the stage for many hellish years to come.

I was bullied. A lot.

Name calling. Beatings. Humiliation. Having stuff stolen. Getting my comics, drawings, and stories taken and torn to shreds. Bullies would rip my stuff apart and torment me, daring me to "do something, pussy."

But I didn't want to do something. I didn't know how to fight, even if I wanted. And I didn't have the capacity for violence in me — yet.

I spent most of my time in middle school, and early high school years, terrified of what might happen on any given day. And the worse it got, the worse my OCD symptoms would crop up — the blinking, the sniffing, the twitching, and all the other things that never stopped racing through my mind.

It felt so random. So hopeless.

I won't go into all of it because I hate dwelling on these things too much or feeling sorry for myself. Some of the worst things I've put behind me and forgotten. But, most importantly, now that I'm older, I understand my bullies and why they did what they did.

It wasn't really about me. It was about them.

I wished I'd understood this when I was a kid.

Maybe I wouldn't have been filled with so much self-loathing and confusion. Things might have been easier because I would've known it wasn't about me. I wouldn't have spent years trying to hide my OCD and the things that made me stand out — I would've embraced them, knowing there was more pain in trying to conform than in just being myself and hoping to eventually find my own fellow freak tribe.

Back then, I felt misunderstood by everyone, especially my family who could never understand why I didn't just stand up for myself. I had tried but wasn't particularly good at hurting people.

And the couple times I did get in a fight, I kinda lost my mind and could've easily killed someone. One time I was bullied, I felt so trapped that I somehow managed to get the better of the kid and dragged him over to a sidewalk, convinced I had to smash his head against it so he couldn't get up and hurt me again.

Thankfully ,my mom intervened and pulled me off the kid.

But that's the level of confinement I felt.

Until I finally found my escape through stories.

2

ESCAPE

I STILL REMEMBER the first comic books I ever got.

I woke up Christmas morning in 1977 to see what Santa had left under the tree.

I had to wait for my parents to wake up before I could open the real gifts. But, as is spelled out in The Parenting Handbook, I could have whatever Santa put in my Christmas stocking.

It's almost as if Santa knew leaving me something to read would give my parents a little longer to sleep.

Inside the stocking was a plastic bag with Marvel's adaptation of Star Wars, issues one through three.

I still remember the cover of that first issue with

more clarity than I remember any other book or comic from my childhood — Luke Skywalker front and center with his lightsaber and an unforgettable scowl. Behind him, Han Solo with his blaster, Princess Leia looking mysterious, Obi-Wan Kenobi with his light saber. Behind them all, the villainous Darth Vader and the Death Star surrounded by a bright glow. Chaos erupting at the sides with X-Wing and TIE fighters buzzing about.

So much action promised in those pages!

Even though I'd seen the movie — because I was a kid in the seventies and, hello, um, Star Wars — I was still excited to revisit the world in the pages of a comic book. Maybe even more than I'd been excited to see it on the big screen.

This was before the days where you could own or stream anything you wanted. Seeing a movie meant going out and standing in line ... with other humans!

Weird, I know.

But this was a chance to hold the world of Star Wars in my hands, to examine every frame, to experience the world again and at my own pace.

It was also my first realization of the escape from reality that story can offer.

This was before I needed the escape. I was relatively happy at age seven, but I was often bored. Being able to open a comic and get a glimpse at worlds imagined by writers and artists that still felt soooooo real was nothing less than amazing.

I could almost feel parts of my brain lighting up for the first time ever.

And as I kept buying and reading issues of Star Wars, I realized something I'd never considered before. Once the comics told the story of the movie, they were probably going to continue with ... new stories!

The Empire Strikes Back wasn't yet a thing.

The comics would be my way to learn what happened next. And oh, man, was I dying to know! I was like a scholar of this fictional world, desperate to learn what might happen next to Luke, Leia, Han, Chewie, and, of course, C-3PO and R2-D2.

I fell in love with the serialized nature of comics. I raced through the pages, eager for, and dreading, those three words: to be continued...

I needed to read MORE comics.

I went from Star Wars to Spider-Man to The Uncanny X-Men to The Avengers to The Incredible Hulk to pretty much any comic I could get my hands on. This was back when you could get a comic for thirty-five cents and the corner convenience store had several rows begging to be bought. I can still remember the smell of my local 7-11 as I scoured the wire rack of covers staring back at me — all the possible worlds and characters, waiting for me to explore them.

But, after I bought a Slurpee — and you can't go to 7-11 as a kid and not get a Slurpee — I only had enough money for one or two comics at most, so I would spend forever trying to make a decision.

I devoted hours to getting lost in those pages and those worlds.

And as I got older and began facing some of the hurdles life tends to throw our way, comics offered an escape from the harshness of reality. They allowed me to face fears of the unknown through these larger-than-life characters, some of them who had the same problems as me. I similarly got lost in old collections of Peanuts books which made me feel less alone because I could relate to the anxieties and insecurities of Charlie Brown and his friends.

As I went into middle and high school and times got tougher, I found Stephen King, Dean Koontz, and a host of other writers who offered me thrilling escapism and a sort of catharsis for my own issues.

They didn't solve my problems magically, but they did something which meant more to me than solutions would have.

They showed me that no matter how much of a freak or an outcast I felt like, I wasn't alone.

These books were filled with other misunderstood rejects, bullied kids, people struggling with mental issues, and heroes battling the darkness. Even if I didn't identify with any of the characters, the stories and worlds offered temporary escape from my real world problems.

That's a powerful realization that could be all the difference between feeling lost and feeling so lost that I couldn't go on. Without comics, books, and their promise of escape, I'm not sure I could have gone on.

By high school, books and comics offered a literal escape. I learned if I didn't go to lunch and instead found a quiet corner away from everyone else where I could read, I was less likely to get noticed.

If the bullies didn't see me, they'd find someone else to pick on.

Sorry to whomever that other target might've been!

As I sat in the halls, hiding away from the world,

my mind on these amazing journeys, something else was happening.

I was no longer content to just read the stories.

I was inspired to create my own.

3

WHY TELL DARK STORIES?

I WAS a bit of a mama's boy.

Since my mother was a stay-at-home mom and I didn't have many friends growing up, I spent most of my time with her. I'm not sure if that's the reason I was a bit more feminine and emotional, or if I was just born that way. At any rate, it didn't do me any favors in making friends with other boys. Girls, on the other hand, I got along with awesomely — which did help me later on. So, thanks, Mom!

Being on the emotional side, I felt things on a deeper level than most of my male friends. Or at least, I felt like I did. More likely they felt things, too, but buried those emotions beneath a veneer of toughness and I don't give a damns.

All of this is to say I tend to feel things deeply.

Sometimes a bit too deeply.

My wife laughs whenever I tear up during sports, a TV show, movie, or ... even a commercial.

"I'm not crying. There's dust and onions in my eyes!"

But feeling too much can be a bit too much at times.

Which is why we need catharsis, a release of strong or repressed emotions.

Ever notice how sometimes you feel good after a good cry?

I'd better not be the only person admitting to this.

That's catharsis!

And while a scary book or a thriller with dark themes might not make you cry, it can provide relief just the same from fear and anxiety.

And once I started writing, I realized the practice allowed me to work through many of my fears and anxieties.

Sean and Johnny like to joke that our horror books tend to feature children in jeopardy.

And yeah, they're right.

But if you were to go back to my writing before I had a child — not that I'd ever finished a book back then — there were zero children in jeopardy.

Most of my scary stories were about people closer to my age, whether I was a teen in school, working graveyard shifts in my twenties, or an adult after that. Their fears tended toward supernatural threats or monsters. I rarely wrote about man's inner demons back then.

Only after I held my son for the first time did I realize the depths of true fear that extend beyond yourself.

It seems like the sort of fear that only a parent — or maybe an older sister or brother of a much younger sibling — can truly understand. I'd become almost hyper-aware of threats to not only my son but even other people's kids when I'm out and about.

I began to see danger everywhere, my Parental Spidey Sense pinging at some kid about to wipe out in a parking lot, fall out of a shopping cart, or run smack into traffic. I could see these things before they were about to happen. My heart would catch in my throat as I was torn between shouting "look out!" and minding my own business because I don't want to be that over-paranoid helicopter parent.

That fear lives in a parent's gut. And when you're me, you mine that fear for story ideas. You intention-ally put children in jeopardy.

I write dark stories for many reasons, and

thrilling audiences is chief among them. But I also do it to offer escape and catharsis, so I can exorcise the things that haunt me.

You might write for another reason. Maybe to shed light on things most people don't see, to work through some past trauma, or to offer an escape and catharsis to your readers.

But first you need to plumb the depths of your darkness.

WHAT IS YOUR DARKNESS?

What are you afraid of?

There are plenty of things to be afraid of in this world. Tune into your 24-hour news channel of choice for a reminder of just how awful the world is all day every day ad infinitum.

In case you don't keep a list of fears in your pocket, you can borrow some of mine:

- War
- Pestilence
- Drowning
- Dying (though most of these have something to do with death)

- Random acts of violence
- Being buried alive
- Getting cancer
- Losing other people to cancer
- Those brain-eating bacteria
- Alzheimer's or dementia
- A deadly fungus we have no protection from
- The dentist
- Running out of Diet Coke/Pepsi
- Really aggressive clowns

AND THAT'S JUST my decoy list.

What, you thought I'd give you my real list of fears? For all I know, you're my arch enemy probing for weaknesses!

Point is, you could take any of those fears, or even mix and match them — a dentist who commits random acts of violence — and have more than enough to build a compelling story around.

But writing your darkness isn't just about fear.

Darkness often festers within trauma and, more importantly, in the effects of that trauma on your characters. It's the things we think about in the dead of night when we're trying to sleep but slumber refuses to come because, damn it, we've got things to worry about and dwell upon.

Authors frequently dig into their pasts, or the histories of their friends and loved ones, to tackle traumatic events. Those stories can offer catharsis to both the author and those who have suffered.

You'd be surprised how much it can help people to see your characters coping with, and perhaps even overcoming, their fears and trauma — their darkness.

I used to write and draw a comic strip called *Todd and Penguin*. It was a cute, family-friendly strip about a talking cookie-loving penguin that lived with a guy named Todd (then later his wife, Holly), and a smart-ass cat, because, as we all know, cats are smart-asses.

Anyway, being a funny, family-friendly comic, what did your pal, Dave decide to do?

Well, I thought it'd be a great idea to do a story-line about a miscarriage.

Yes, you read that right — a miscarriage.

I know, hilarious subject matter, right?

I'd written the story in response to my father-in-law's struggle with cancer. It wasn't a one-to-one representation of his ordeal, or even about cancer. I try not to write so much about actual happenings in my life or those in the lives around me, but about the emotions within those events. So while my storyline wasn't about cancer, it was about losing family and how fate doesn't give a damn about our plans.

As one might think, I had a few reservations about that storyline.

One reader later spoke of the storyline being so out of left field that it was like finding a brutal murder spree storyline playing out in the Garfield comic strip.

I would totally read that comic, by the way. Or write it, Jim Davis, if you're looking for a collaborator.

Anyway, you don't typically expect such serious topics like miscarriage in a light comic that more often makes people go "awww" than bust their gut laughing. I might have even been the first light comic to go so dark, back in 2002 or 2003.

But sometimes when you fear writing about something, it means you should.

So I did.

I was afraid of many things. First, that I'd built up Todd and Holly's pregnancy into this thing. People were looking forward to the baby! I had all these cute and funny storylines involving Penguin dealing with the baby and Oscar hating it (because Oscar's a cat and he hates everything).

I hadn't planned for this and had done nothing to prepare readers for the coming gut punch.

Second, I was afraid that someone who'd actually had a miscarriage (I hadn't, though, in a cruel twist of fate, my wife and I would a few years later) would see the storyline as a cheap trick or exploitation of actual tragedy.

But I couldn't write about cancer in that moment, the actual tragedy we were facing. So, I transferred it to something that felt safer for us. Of course, it wasn't. But you can't always plan for how everybody will translate your work in their heads.

I felt sick to my stomach as I pushed publish on that first comic, afraid I'd alienate readers or that it was too damned serious and depressing. It wasn't a punchline; the comic was an honest, deep exploration of grief.

The storyline was going to last a good two weeks.

That is a long ass time for a daily comic to maintain such a dark story.

But my wife, her sisters, and all the family were going through a tough time, and I needed some way to process everything in a way that was in my control.

So, I did it.

And, to this date, it's the comic I've gotten the most email about. Many readers even thanked me for writing sensitively about such a difficult subject, including a few who had lost their own children through miscarriage (or worse).

They said my comic helped them. As a creator, that meant more to me than anything else. Through my grieving, my catharsis, I helped other people to heal — just as my favorite creators have always done for me.

WHY DO YOU want to write dark stories?

It's good to think about your personal story and how it relates to your fiction. Dig into your own darkness and find the parallels in your fiction. Find what you're trying to say about the world and our place in it.

Even if you're not sure how you feel about things, you can still explore them in your fiction in a way that will resonate with your readers. Somebody might even need that exact message in their life at that moment to help them get through their darkness.

4

EXPLORING THE DARKNESS

IF YOU'RE WRITING about dark subjects, you probably have strong emotions about the topics you're exploring. Those emotions can help you connect to your characters and craft a better story.

Knowing what a character is going through helps you tell a better, more believable, narrative.

If it's something you've gone through, you can probably tap into those feelings more easily.

I know in my case, when it comes to being bullied, those feelings are always just under the surface, waiting. So are the feelings of being ostracized and misunderstood. And those emotions help in telling stories that have to do with bullying, but they aid me telling other kinds of stories, as well.

Feeling misunderstood is something many

people go through, even those who aren't bullied. Tapping into that lone emotion can help add depth to a character, even if he or she isn't suffering any other effects of bullying.

It can be therapeutic to write about the things that haunt us. Only by examining the darkness can we heal or learn from what happened. Whether it's something we went through or a hurt we caused another, we all have darkness inside us.

It affects our life and our fiction whether we want it to or not, so choose to lean in and be a more intentional artist to get more out of both.

But what if you're writing about something you haven't been through?

EXPLORING OTHER PEOPLES' DARKNESS

If you're writing about a subject you're not personally familiar with, you'll want to research the topic so your story feels authentic. You don't need to become an expert in the field, but the key details need to be right. Also, you want to know how the darkness your character is suffering would affect their life.

You could wing some things, but doing so runs the risk of you minimizing real suffering.

People distressed by mental illness, trauma, or any of the other essential elements of darker fiction don't want to see tragedy used as fodder or as a cheap ploy or plot point. They want a meaningful, or at least decent, story.

That means getting the details right.

Talk to people with experience. Find experts to interview. If you read a magazine article or a book on a subject that interests you, investigate the citations. Join HARO (help a reporter out) and put out a call. Ask questions on Quora. It's never been easier to get the truth if you're willing to look for it.

Read some basic psychology books. Investigate a few of the better self-help titles out there, those delving deep into topics ranging from mental illness to abuse to crime. The more you understand, the better your work will be. This isn't something you learn and move on from; it's a prism through which you view the world to elevate your work. And that's a perspective that's always worth feeding.

Read biographies and online posts. Watch documentaries and YouTube videos of accounts from or about people who are going through what your character will be going through. If you're curious, there's a good chance you can find an existing conversation around the topic. Though there's still a stigma around some issues, particularly mental health, many people are coming forward to share their stories because they see the power in sharing and the power of being less alone.

Always respect those who are sharing their lives with you or the world.

Never co-opt someone else's pain or life for your story. Your job is to tell a story as authentically as you can without lifting another person's experience for your book.

Your character should be your creation.

You just want enough details of similar things people have gone through without telling that person's story. Go through many accounts to find the common elements that will create a general representation rather than a copy and paste experience.

While diving into your research, consider some opposition.

If there's a bad guy in your story, investigate what made them that way. Monsters are made more than born.

Our book, *12*, focuses on twelve hours in twelve lives leading up to a mass shooting. We've been praised for how we wrote one of the most reprehensible characters possible — a pedophile who has kidnapped a child.

We wrote him not as some larger than life monster, but as an abused man whose life has led to his fall. As much as he's the monster in this story, the character is also the victim of his own narrative. That humanity made him even scarier.

When you have a character like that, it's almost easy to believe the bad guy will get his in the end. Because that's how fiction usually works. But when you tell the story of a human who also happens to be a monster, it makes the reader uncertain of what he might be capable of.

That fear makes the story that much more believable. And tense.

If you're writing about a topic with several sides, research them all.

Let's say you've got a rich developer trying to get the local government to declare eminent domain on an impoverished neighborhood so he can build a new shopping center.

And let's say your main story is about a family fighting to stay in their home. That's an easy story to tell, and you can find tons of real life inspiration of people screwed over by both industry and the government acting for "the better good."

Those characters are relatable.

But what if you also understood the developer?

What if you did some research to find their motivation, beyond the presumed greed?

The villain in real life is almost never the villain in their own story. They are the hero. Even if they're misguided as all hell, even if their methods are downright diabolical, they have reasons for doing what they do.

Learning those reasons can help you write more well-rounded characters.

And that makes for a better story that your readers will get lost in.

5

THE PAST IS NEVER THROUGH WITH US

THINGS THAT HAPPEN to us have a way of lingering for a long time, shaping our lives, how we view others, and the world at large.

Victims of trauma, especially in early childhood, often suffer their entire lives, sometimes in unexpected ways. A loud noise might send someone with Post Traumatic Stress Disorder into a full-blown panic attack. Smelling a scent or seeing something might trigger reminders of past abuse. These things can make normal life quite difficult. A simple trip to the mall can be a dangerous minefield of triggers.

Consider how trauma might shape your character.

Perhaps your character experienced something awful early in her life. As a kid, she was outgoing and destined for great things. But then something happened. Afterward, she starts to shut herself off from others, doesn't trust easily, and has a difficult time finding friends or loves. Because she blames herself, she's self-loathing and self-destructive. Maybe she takes a job that's beneath her just to avoid other people or particular situations related to her trauma.

There is an infinite number of ways trauma can change us and our lives forever.

Victims of abuse often suffer from PTSD that changes them in profound ways. PTSD affects everybody differently and often requires years of therapy or a combination of therapy and medication to cope.

In Lynne Ramsay's *You Were Never Really Here*, Ramsay takes what might be a typical thriller plot about a military vet named Joe rescuing girls from girls from sex trafficking and adds a layer of PTSD which fundamentally upgrades the story to something beyond the regular. And, depending on your interpretation of the movie's events, it could change Joe's motivations dramatically.

I don't want to spoil the story if you've not seen it, but Joe isn't just some wise-cracking bad ass killer of reprehensible criminals trafficking in sex slaves, including children. He is deeply scarred with some serious psychological wounds.

You can feel his past and his pain in his every movement and glance. In the things he does and how he reacts to each situation. His life has been carved by abuse, and it adds so much to the almost non-existent plot that you feel the movie on a deep level. Sure, that feeling might be a punch in the gut, but damn, it's effective.

Because it's authentic.

You know Joe has seen some shit. As the movie progresses, you get glimpses of his past that make you that much more invested in whether he can save the child he's been hired to find and what happens to him.

Real-life heroes aren't flashy, in-your-face action stars. That character works in the blockbusters, but if you want your audience to feel something more, you can't give them cardboard or clones. Your readers, and your characters, deserve depth, and that's often born from suffering.

Another stellar example of using trauma to elevate a story beyond its premise is Netflix's *The Haunting of Hill House*.

Mike Flanagan took Shirley Jackson's classic ghost story — widely viewed as one of the best haunted house stories ever written — and made a series that's better than the prior movie versions and all the imitators that followed.

This version of *The Haunting of Hill House* dived deep into the psyches of the family living in Hill House, exploring their lives both as kids in the past and adults in the present. The mysteries of the house are only part of the story, though. The show depicts the longterm effects of the trauma the kids endured, how it shaped their lives, and how it changed them into the adults they are.

Those effects continue to play out in the present with these characters all struggling with something. And with one another.

Their struggles make us care so much about them.

I'd have loved the show even if there was no supernatural element. I felt for them in a way few TV shows have made me feel.

That is the power of darkness in your story — making people care.

Making them feel connected to your characters as if they're living, breathing people with their own pasts, fears, loves, and desires.

We've all experienced hardships, but only through story can we connect to the hardships of others. Fiction makes us more empathetic toward other people.

Think about how gay people used to be depicted in fiction — as perverts and rapists. Feared as an unknown, as evil. As "Other." Racist, homophobic, and anti-Semitic propaganda relies on perpetuating these fears of some very different "Other."

But fiction from authors who are different from us, peopled with characters who are different from us, portrayed by actors and actresses who are different from us has shown us how similar we all truly are.

When we can connect through shared joys and miseries, we can connect as people. We see that Other isn't truly all that different from us after all. We see beyond the lies that seek to divide us.

And given how much divisiveness there is in the world today — and maybe always has been — anything that brings us together can't be all that bad.

6

HOW TO EXPLORE THE DARKNESS
WITHOUT GETTING LOST IN IT

How do you explore such dark territories (within your own psyche or outside yourself) without it overwhelming you?

I've written some grim stories. How grim you ask?

Sean likes to claim I'm on a personal mission to see just how far I can push him until he cries mercy.

He has to edit my work and write to my outlines.

Our collaboration usually follows one of these methods:

1. I write the first draft of a story then send it to him.

2. He writes the first draft and then sends it to me.

3. I, or both of us, outline a story for him to write.

IN EVERY SITUATION, Sean has to read something I wrote, either for myself or for him. But Sean's not as dark as I am. He's like me as a kid, an optimistic, lovable puppy dog, always wanting to believe in the best of people.

I, on the other hand, am like one of those junk-yard dogs chained to a tree or a brick. I've seen the worst of people. When I see a stranger, my first instinct is to growl. I am not prone to seeing the best in people.

Sean is so focused on filling his head with positive things, he mostly ignores the news and the horrors of the world around us. He fights to keep his optimism intact.

I can't stop thinking of terrible shit that can go wrong. Part of it comes from my childhood and losing people I loved to early deaths. Part of it is my time as a reporter constantly seeing the worst in people. And a big part of it is the constant OCD and anxious chatter in my head telling me all the things that can end my world in an instant.

My mind is so fertile with horrible things that if

there were an Olympic sport for thinking up worst case scenarios, I'd win gold. Every single time. No matter what misery-drenched athlete they brought up against me to think up something bad, I'd think up something worse, by leaps and bounds.

Sometimes when I'm writing, I might go a bit further into darker areas than I would on my own just to shock the hell out of Sean.

SEE! This is the real world! Look at it! Behold!

When I'm writing, I rely on his optimism to reign in my worst case scenarios.

Dave, maybe all the kids on the bus don't die in this story, okay?

Okay, Sean. Good call.

Sometimes, though, Sean fails to save me from my darkness.

Sometimes, he'll go even darker.

I suspect he's having so much fun exploring the dark side with me, that he'll say, hell, why not kill all the kids on all the buses!

I sometimes think he's trying to get readers mad at me.

Oh, look what horrible thing Dave wrote this time! It couldn't have been Sean; he's too sweet!

Last year I was writing a first draft of a story

where I needed to give our characters a miserable back story. The thing that made the most sense to me for these particular characters was that they lost their infant child.

Not just lost their infant child, but lost their infant child on Christmas morning.

Sean immediately sent me a message in our company chat and asked, "Dude, WTF? On CHRISTMAS? We can't have a dead baby on Christmas!"

I wasn't aware we had a No Dead Babies on Christmas rule, but apparently we do.

Sean said, "the reader feels the emotion with the loss of their baby, Christmas morning makes it misery porn."

The story has yet to see publication. It had other problems than being too dark, but yeah, that's a glimpse of how black I can get.

I write about pain because it's a part of everyone's life. It's cathartic for me. Keeping it all inside is far worse and only adds to my anxiety and depression.

But there are times that writing in the dark can be overwhelming, even for me.

So, back to the question — how do you keep that darkness from overwhelming you?

It depends on what kind of writer you are.

Some writers always keep some distance between themselves and their characters and story. They see it all as this big fiction and it doesn't really affect them.

Other writers, like me, get more in-depth with what our characters are feeling or going through.

If they are in pain, we're in pain. If they're embarrassed after a bad date, a part of us is cringing. If they're suffering the sting of loss, we feel it, too. Some actors are method actors, behaving like their character even off-set. We're method writers.

I'm not saying we need to feel exactly what our characters feel. I don't want to know exactly what every monster I write about feels like.

Well, if I'm gonna write about a serial killer who kills his victims using nothing but LEGO bricks, I'd better get busy!

But I can use my imagination and find a parallel, a safe distance away from becoming a monster myself. I might not be able to get in the exact head space of a teacher shooting his students (*WhiteSpace*), but I've seen interviews with madmen and have met scary paranoid people.

If we see the bad guy from his perspective, we

can usually find something to help us make some sense of the senseless.

The villain is usually the hero of their own story. So, ask yourself how he sees the situation. How did he get to this point? What does he believe that would cause him to ignore his own morality? Or what happened to him that would remove the barriers most of us have? How does he justify it to himself? Or maybe he can't.

Sometimes there is no reason that makes sense to anybody, or it's a reason so buried that nobody knows. But even if your characters don't understand why things are happening, you as the writer should.

PLAYING PRETEND

I used to love playing with my Star Wars figures. It's where I discovered the magic of making shit up.

I'd craft long and elaborate stories about the characters before playing them out for hours on end. I'd even end my sessions with a to be continued ... and pick up the storyline later.

More often than not, I'd pretend the characters weren't Star Wars characters but actually heroes and villains I'd made up myself. There weren't many good Marvel or DC action figures at the time, so I'd play with the closest thing I could find.

In my stories, Boba Fett wasn't the bounty hunter we know, but a super hero in a cool ass suit, not unlike Iron Man.

It's funny how much playing with action figures is like writing to me.

Much of what I do is lining up characters in my head and acting out scenarios. I don't act them all out or use action figures. And if I did, I sure as hell wouldn't admit that to you.

If you don't have a lot of personal darkness to tap into or you're writing about something you've not experienced, use your imagination.

Imagine the worst things that can happen to you instead of your characters. How would you react?

That's just the starting point.

Now how would you react if you were your character (who, I assume, isn't too much like you)?

Depending on their life experiences, their resources, and mental state, they might handle the same situation in a very different way than you or I would.

There's a lot of playing pretend, but diving deeper into each of your characters, at least the ones you want people to remember, is never wasted time.

But it can take its toll on you. Or on your collaborator, if you write with someone like me. So, how do
you get out of that headspace?

This is only my third time asking the question, I
really ought to answer it by now, eh?

Not quite yet.

I still remember when I was researching car accidents for our book, *Crash*.

I've been at a number of crash scenes over the
years, including the most heart wrenching one
where me and my friend arrived first at a scene
where a man transporting giant cement sewage
pipes stopped short to avoid a car that cut him off.
The cement pipes broke free and crushed him to
death.

I remember going up to the truck's crumpled cab
to see if he was okay, holding out hope that
somehow he hadn't been crushed.

The door was bent outward, blood flowing out of
it and onto the road.

I could not get the door open even if I'd wanted
to. And I didn't want to see what was waiting
behind it.

But I'd not seen an actual dead body in a
crash. And our character in that story is
obsessed with photographing accidents. We

needed authenticity, things he would undoubtedly notice.

Let's just say I would've been better off imagining that little detail.

I came across a video uploaded to a popular site that posts news and user-submitted videos of car crashes. This one wasn't just a car crash, but some European crash involving at least a few dozen cars. And whoever was recording the video walked among the dead and dying, recording them.

Not helping, just recording.

It still haunts me.

So, back to the question, (Oh, you're finally going to answer it, Dave?) how do you not lose yourself to the overwhelming sadness in such subjects? Especially when you're researching horrible events with real people dying?

It's difficult.

I've talked to several police officers and first responders to ask them how they manage to push the worst days out of their heads.

Many of them have difficulty doing it. They tell me you do whatever it takes to cope. Some will hug their kids. Others adopt gallows humor, finding whimsy in terrible things because it's the only way to cope without cracking. Some drink to forget.

Not comparing what we're doing on the page to what these people have to see in real life, but my advice is similar. Do whatever it takes to cope. Except the drinking part, which your liver might hate you for.

I might make a joke to Sean in the notes of my draft. For instance, for the dead baby at Christmas, I might say, "Happy Christmas to all, and to all a good night!" with an image of Santa or something.

I always try and find some good thing in the story, a glimmer of hope where there isn't one in real life. Again, I'm not writing about actual things. It would be far more difficult for me to do that if I was writing non-fiction stories about people that really suffered these horrors.

But, as a fiction writer, I can find some light in the darkness.

Beyond the page, I take breaks as often as I can whenever I'm writing something particularly dark. The important thing is to change your surroundings. Just getting up from the chair can do wonders for your mindset.

Going for a walk usually helps me re-center. So does spending time with friends or family, playing a quick video game, or finding something light on TV, like a mindless sitcom or romantic comedy. Whatever you enjoy.

A change of scenery and getting out of your own head is the most important part about not succumbing to the nature of our darkest work.

7

LET'S RUIN A LIFE TOGETHER

THIS IS the chapter I was most excited to write in this book. Now, we're in my wheelhouse — thinking up really terrible shit on top of already heinous atrocities.

Story is about creating tension.

Writing dark stories, especially thrillers, is about continuing to tighten the screws until the reader (and the characters) can no longer take it. It's that moment when you think it can't get any more hopeless for the character then it does!

You think they can't possibly get out of this mess, but relief is delivered when that character somehow uses their smarts or skills or overcome some personal issue to save the day.

But where do you start such a story?

I like to start with a well-rounded, believable character and focus on his or her internal and external conflicts. So let's start there and ruin a life together.

Don't worry, it'll be a character's life, not a real life. Though, I'm sure if you're creative, you could think up some ways to do that, too. Just leave me out of that one, please.

For now, let's brainstorm a character then destroy her life.

Sound like fun?

Let's go!

We'll call our main character Rachel.

Normally, when I'm fleshing out a character, I'll come up with the basics.

What is she like?

How old is she?

What's her job?

What does she look like?

Is she married?

Does she have kids?

What does she do for fun?

What are her fears?

What secrets is she keeping and why?

But for now, let's just focus on what's wrong with her.

Her internal conflict is the thing that's wrong with her that she's trying to overcome. Let's say she's addicted to pills. Sean would say we've used that trope a lot, but hey, addiction is something I understand and have lost people to, so why not tap into that part of my darkness?

You will have your own darkness you can tap into, and your story will be different.

But for now, let's brainstorm this one using my darkness.

Rachel is an addict, struggling to put her life back together. She was sober for a good amount of time, but then she slipped. We'll come back to that in a minute.

Insert evil smile.

That's a good start, but let's dig deeper.

What caused her to become addicted? Everybody has an origin story, the Big Thing that really messed them up. What happened to Rachel?

Maybe she was abused by a trusted family member. Maybe her uncle.

Maybe she even went to her parents and told them, but they didn't believe her. Maybe they even punished her for lying about her uncle.

All of these make for a complex backstory, and each layer you add can offer twists and turns to her ongoing relationships. Because nothing happens in a vacuum. Rachel would still have resentment toward her family. Maybe that's a B story going on as your A story unfolds — dealing with one of her parents, or even the abuser.

We've got the internal conflict down, so let's move onto the external conflict.

Since we (and yes, I mean we because if you're reading this far, you're a co-conspirator with me) like putting children in jeopardy, we'll say your main character's son is kidnapped. We'll stick with the R's and call her son Rob. He's in fourth grade, old enough to maybe walk home from school alone since it's only a block away, but she always goes to meet him anyway.

Here's where knowing her internal conflict, addiction, pays off. We customize the bad thing that happens to her so it's because of her internal conflict. That way we can truly squeeze her and ruin her life!

Let's say she had a relapse and that led to her son being taken. She passed out from her pills and missed picking her kid up from school.

He decided to walk home.

And that was the last time anyone ever saw him.

Imagine how much that would tear Rachel up. Not only was her child taken, but she's to blame. Guilt is a great punisher and motivator.

Now we have the internal and external conflict. A mother with a missing child. And her addiction is partially responsible for her son's abduction.

What else can we do to destroy her?

What roadblocks custom designed to her particular darkness can we throw in her way?

What if the boy's father, her ex-husband, is a cop? We'll call him Jack.

And they had a terrible custody fight. Jack knew of her drug use before. Maybe he even had custody until she proved she was clean for a year. Now he's suspicious of her again. He wants her to submit to a drug test. If she fails, he would make sure she never got Rob back when — if — they somehow get the kid from the kidnappers.

At this point you're probably thinking, "Man, Rachel is screwed!"

Yes, but this is a story, and we need to keep tightening those screws.

What else can we do to mess with her?

I'm not saying this as some sort of monster that

enjoys when my characters suffer. If I'm really into the story and the characters, I feel their pain. But, as I said, I do take pride in thinking up horrible things for my character to overcome.

Now we've got our protagonist, Rachel.

And we've got a couple of antagonists. We've got the unknown kidnapper, and we've got Jack. And yes, Jack is a cop, and by most accounts, a decent guy, but he's the antagonist for the purposes of this story. Why?

Because the thing he wants, custody of Rob, is the same thing our protagonist wants. And they can't both have custody. Maybe she lives in another state or Jack's schedule is such that he can't spend enough quality time with the child. While they could both have custody, Rachel feels it's not in Rob's interest for him to stay with his dad.

But they do have a shared goal of finding Rob.

They could work together in an uneasy truce to find out what happened to their son. But even if they are working together, does Rachel trust Jack? Should she?

Maybe he's looking for reasons to ensure she never gets Rob back? Maybe this whole story can be a way to push both of them past their limits before they can overcome whatever differences they had to renew their friendship or their love.

But not yet.

First, we need more bad shit to happen.

What if Rachel has a boyfriend with a shady past. A boyfriend that gave her the drugs? That would put Rachel in a tight spot and be another thing for her and Jack to clash over.

What if the boyfriend actually does have something to do with Rob's disappearance? Maybe Rachel has some money and the dealer is being squeezed by some bad people for money. He can't just go to her and ask, so he arranges this fake kidnapping.

Man, Rachel is not having luck in the Men Department!

In any event, it's all trouble for Rachel as her world is falling apart.

Now we can kick in with the B story. Perhaps in an effort to find her son, she has to go to her estranged mother or father for help. Maybe her father knows people who can help. An unsavory lot for sure, but the sort of folks who would know the kind of guys who took her kid. But first, she has to overcome the hate she feels for her parents for not believing her, for standing by the uncle.

What if we can even tie the uncle into this story?

What if he's the guy squeezing her boyfriend?

Or what if he's somehow taken the kid from the people that had the kid just to get control over Rachel?

Maybe to silence her? Or maybe he's got even worse plans for the kid?

Can you see how much more all of this matters because of the personal stakes to Rachel?

It's not just another missing kid story. It has layers because of Rachel's past and the darkness she's dealing with.

If we dig a bit deeper we could turn this into one hell of a story, maybe even a smash hit movie, especially if we can bake in a mystery with a hell of a twist tied directly to Rachel's conflicts. Or maybe we could even turn it into a long-running, beloved HBO series which would amaze everybody right up until the last season!

And, if you're anything like me, you're probably thinking a lot about Rachel right now. Maybe even worrying about what's going to happen to her. I hope you're not feeling too down, though. If so, you can always take the advice from the previous chapter and go for a walk or something.

But if you're really like me, you'll probably wind up somewhere between being relaxed and thinking of even more things that can go wrong for Rachel. In which case, bring something to record those ideas for your book!

8

OVERCOMING THE DARKNESS

YOU MIGHT BE WONDERING why we're making our character jump through so many damned hoops. Why make things more difficult as the story progresses? Are we masochists who enjoy inflicting pain on fictional creations?

No.

Well, you might be, but I'm not judging.

There is a point to the suffering, though. Your character's journey has to mean something to them if it's going to mean something to your reader.

We've all read books or seen movies where the hero or heroine saves the day or survives the monsters, but we're still left unsatisfied, maybe even saying to ourselves, "Well, that happened. That was, technically, a book I read."

But the story has no meaning for us.

Why? Because the character didn't overcome, or at least confront, their darkness. Maybe they found some *deus ex machina* that happened to conveniently help them save the day. But it wasn't an earned victory. It was cheap. They didn't achieve it through any of their own choices or actions.

The story shouldn't be a thing that happens to our characters. They need agency. Good or bad, they should experience impact through their choices.

When your character survives not only against all odds but against their personal darkness, that story will resonates with us, and be the kind we remember and tell our friends about.

We're all warring with something, and we like to see people win those wars because maybe, just maybe, it means we can, too.

Yes, even fictional characters overcoming adversity can inspire us because they remind us what's at stake. Stories put things into perspective and provide us with an idea or motivation to fight our own darkness.

Stories have the power to transform our lives.

.   .   .

WHY CREATE DARK CHARACTERS IN THE FIRST PLACE?

We create dark characters, in part, to pose a threat to our hero, but also to show the world as it exists in all its complexity. Even if the world is some fantasy realm that doesn't exist, the author of the story is likely using this other world in an attempt to depict humanity and all its flaws since it's sometimes easier to show us what we're like by using people who aren't exactly like us.

Dark characters aren't just reserved for your villains. Some of the most memorable heroes in fiction today are struggling with dark sides. The classic alcoholic detective struggling with sobriety, the brooding anti-hero who refuses to ask for help, the demon hunter haunted by her past — giving your hero flaws makes them more relatable and therefore interesting to your reader.

Introducing darkness to your character adds to the number of threats. They don't have to just worry about the enemy but also about some element of themselves lurking in the B story.

Might this be the moment where your alcoholic detective relapses and endangers not only the case, but other people's lives?

Might your brooding anti-hero's inability to

connect push someone he cares about right into the arms of danger?

Might your demon hunter's past fears come to surface at the exact moment she needs her wits to save the day?

The best stories are those where the hero faces two enemies, the external and the internal. The better you write them, the greater the stakes will be and the more uncertainty your reader will feel about whether your hero is up to the battle with such unsurmountable odds stacked against them.

MAKE ME CARE

Horror, when done well, is my absolute favorite genre. But when done poorly, it's my least favorite. It's embarrassingly bad, and I can understand why so many people look down on it — because they haven't seen examples of horror done right.

And for a horror story to work, it needs one thing above all else — people we care about. Don't give me some story about a random group of college kids getting sliced and diced at a summer camp and expect me not to root for the masked killer.

If you want me to cheer for the heroes, make me

care. Give them qualities I can relate to. Make them feel like living, breathing people.

One of my favorite horror movies, Neil Marshall's *The Descent*, did this perfectly.

If you look at the synopsis — six women spelunking in a cave system get trapped with monsters underground — you'd probably think, "Okay, I've seen this movie."

But unless you've seen *The Descent,* you haven't seen this particular movie.

Why? Because *The Descent* does something that so many awful, instantly forgettable horror movies and novels fail to do — it invests in the characters.

When an author invests in the characters, so will the audience.

These aren't just six friends on a trip that goes terribly wrong. It's a movie that slowly reveals Sarah's past tragedy. Secrets boil under the surface (internal conflict), about to explode as the characters find themselves in the battle of their lives against these scary as hell creatures in very dark and confined spaces (external conflict).

Sarah is forced to make tough choices as she and her friends try to survive the ordeal.

Backstory informs the characters' present in

such a way that viewers demand to know more. It's a devastating moment once they do.

You want your readers to bond with your characters, so they need to see and feel at least some of what your heroes are going through. The more connected your readers are to the characters, the more they'll feel and believe it when you put those characters in danger.

But writing a dark story isn't about heaping endless amounts of misery upon our characters. You want to balance bad with good to effectively build tension.

We'll talk about how to do that in the next chapter.

9

HOW MUCH IS TOO MUCH? SPACING OUT YOUR DARKNESS

THERE's a difference in telling a dark story and something that is both bleak and unrelenting. It's a fine line, and one many people disagree on.

I don't like movies that deliver punch after punch until the viewer feels nothing. Beat me into submission and I will submit ... and stop caring.

We've all seen the kind of movie I'm talking about.

Oh, and now another person I don't care about was gruesomely killed. What's next?

Those movies are even worse when they end on a bleak note. Take for instance, a movie I was very much looking forward to. But when I saw it in the theater, I felt empty at the end — as if I'd witnessed actual murders.

Big spoilers for 2008's *The Strangers* incoming:

BEGIN SPOILERS

BRYAN BERTINO'S *The Strangers* was a home invasion movie I wanted to like.

It starred Liv Tyler (Kristen) and Scott Speedman (James), a couple staying at a vacation house in a secluded area. Then masked strangers show up and terrorize the couple over the course of the entire movie.

The Strangers did a fantastic job at building tension. I can't recall if the movie did the hard work of giving the characters a decent backstory or inner conflict. I can barely remember movies I saw last year, let alone more than a decade ago. But it built tension well. A little too well, as it seemed to only get more vicious as it went, with no relief in my memory.

It was difficult to watch, partly because it was unrelenting in its horror and partly because of the randomness of the crime. The movie did a great job of capturing a primal fear of just how random violence can be.

The movie ends with Kristen and James tied up, helpless.

When the strangers removed their masks, Kristen asked why they were doing this.

One of the characters, Dollface, replied, "Because you were home."

Then the strangers stabbed the couple and left them for dead.

It's a brutal ending of what seemed like a random thrill-kill. And it's a hard movie to get catharsis from because I was left with the question, "Why did I waste two hours on this only to watch the main characters die?"

The movie teases that Kristen survived the attack, but it's not clear that she truly lives or only keeps breathing long enough to give one last jump scare to the audience.

END SPOILERS

I DON'T HATE the movie. Nor do I hate all movies with dark endings. But there has to be something else in it for me beyond bleak, unrelenting misery. *The Strangers* just wasn't for me. Bertino has since directed, written, or produced (or all three) quite a few movies I enjoyed.

But *The Strangers* left me feeling empty, and while there's certainly a place for that kind of book or movie, it will always be a much smaller audience.

And if you deliver too many experiences like that, you might scare away everyone except those people who appreciate especially bleak material.

I try to aim for dark stuff with a ray of hope. That's where I believe most of my readers like to spend their time, in the darkness but with light bleeding into the horizon. Those the sorts of stories I most enjoy.

So how do you keep from getting too dark?

ADDING LIGHT MOMENTS AND HUMOR

Vary your story's pace to give the reader moments of respite to break up the tension. If you go full-speed with an avalanche of non-stop atrocities, the audience becomes numb.

They need down time. A chance to recalibrate and catch their breath, even if it's only so you can scare it out of them again in a few minutes.

It's these quiet moments between the action

beats you can use to add character development and make your reader care more about them.

I like to add a bit of levity in these moments.

In our story *Available Darkness*, there's a quiet moment near the end where our heroes are about to go to war against the enemy. But first, they stop off at a McDonald's where Abigail (our very first child in jeopardy!) is introduced to the joy of dipping French Fries into a chocolate milkshake.

This sets off a culinary debate between John, our silent and serious protagonist, and his sidekicks, Larry and Tiny.

It's a scene played for light laughs, but it also serves as a moment where they get to take a pause in the action (along with the readers) and bond a bit as they realize some of them might not make it out of the battle alive.

It also sets up the next scene, a tender moment where John, who had been a bit gruff with Abigail, gets a teddy bear from a gas station and gives it to her, showing a caring side he'd been pushing down prior to that point in the story.

This scene makes us care more about both John and Abigail before things get scary. The quiet interlude allows us to remind our readers of the stakes before all hell breaks loose, without a bunch of

exposition. The relationships between these characters is made all the more real with the humor and
touching moments.

USING HUMOR TO BALANCE

Every cook will prepare a dish differently
according to their tastes, same as authors use the
spice of humor according to either their preference
or genre expectation.

I use it sparingly because most of our books tend
to have a darker mood. And I don't like to undercut
the seriousness of the story by having the characters
joking their way through the narrative. The humor
must be natural to the story and character or it will
feel shoehorned in and undermine the scene's
integrity. I also find that using humor sparingly
makes those moments much richer or funnier.

Sean and I often disagree on humor in our
books, but one example where he thought it was
appropriate is perhaps one of his best calls in our
writing history.

Our big post-apocalyptic serial, *Yesterday's Gone*,
was the first book we truly collaborated on. We
wrote *Available Darkness* first, but it was mostly my
story. Sean didn't do any of the first draft writing or

planning since parts of it had been with me since I was young.

Yesterday's Gone was our first book together where we both created and wrote.

We began with a premise — what if a group of strangers woke up and found everybody else in the world was gone?

We began with only that concept, neither of us knowing where it would go beyond that.

We each created a handful of characters on our own then ran with half of the first episode of the series — writing our groups of survivors of the mysterious Event completely independent of each other.

It's a crazy way to co-write a book, but we were pioneers, bringing serials to the e-book revolution. And, besides, it didn't need to be perfect on the first draft. We'd make sense of it all in our follow-up passes. We were writing on a tightrope, and it was both scary and awesome.

I didn't want to go into it completely blind, so before we started writing, I asked Sean what kinds of characters he had written, basically a loose sketch of the kinds of people he'd have in his chapters. I didn't want to echo his character types and wanted different sorts of people populating our world.

I came up with a journalist looking for his missing wife and son, a man who is either part of a secret government task force or a delusional threat, a pregnant teenage girl with overly strict parents, a bullied teenage boy, and ... a serial killer.

Sean had come up with a single mother and daughter, an entrepreneur who might know some things about what was going on, a child left all alone who runs into a talking dog, and ... a serial killer.

Yes, we'd both come up with serial killers.

At this point I decided the odds of there being two serial killers among this small of a group (not including people we'd meet later) were pretty slim.

I mean, there's probably only one, maybe two, serial killers on your block.

And I figured my group of characters were enough for me to play with — especially the man who may or may not be a secret agent, so I ditched my serial killer and Sean went with his.

That might be the best decision we've ever made as writers.

Because his serial killer went on to become our most well-known (and notorious) character, Boricio Wolfe. And it's a damned good thing Sean wrote Boricio in the first book or two (and co-wrote him in later ones) because he made him the most ridiculous over-the-top batshit crazy, foul-mouthed walking id of a character I've ever seen.

My serial killer would've been dark and humorless.

Sean played Boricio as audacious and insane. And readers love him. We get emails all the time which read something like, "I know I'm not supposed to, but I love Boricio!"

The person will often add some extra reason they shouldn't love him, pointing out that they're a grandmother or great-grandmother, or that they're this super nice or religious person, and yet ... they still like Boricio. They're almost apologetic about it, which always makes me smile.

I think Boricio worked so well because he's such a unique character. Had we written every character in such an over-the-top manner, the series would've never gone on to be the huge success it's been for us. It would've been too campy, and I'm not a fan of camp.

The character works because he stands out and sprinkles some much needed comic relief among all the horrible happenings — even when Boricio himself is the cause.

So, how much humor should you use? Sean and Johnny use it as an element in most of their books, no matter how sober the story might otherwise be. It all depends on your tastes and that of your audience.

Write the thing you want to read most. That passion will show in your work and will, eventually, appeal to other like-minded readers.

Don't be afraid to experiment. It's your meal, and you're the master chef. Pay attention to what your readers say in email or reviews. They will always let you know if your humor isn't working.

10

DARKNESS TRANSFORMS US

WHETHER IT'S external or internal, darkness transforms our characters. Overcoming the darkness is the point of most stories. Even if your audience isn't conscious of the question, they are constantly asking themselves how the hero will rise to the occasion.

Maybe they won't. There could be transformation in that story, too.

But we usually enjoy tales about people overcoming the odds. And your hero should be changed by events of the story.

How did victory change your hero?

What lessons did they learn? What inner conflict/darkness did they need to overcome to achieve victory?

M. Night Shyamalan's *Signs* offers a great

example of darkness (in the form of grief) transforming its main character. Even better, it shows how he overcomes his darkness, and that transformation saves the day.

Mel Gibson stars as Graham Hess, a former minister who lives with his two children and younger brother on a remote farm when aliens arrive. Most of the extraterrestrial threat plays out on TV reports, adding to the fear this family feels as danger closes in.

Signs, like the more recent, *A Quiet Place*, is basically a smarter, smaller alien invasion movie that focuses more on the characters of one family than a sprawling cast like the kind found in a popcorn flick like *Independence Day*.

Because *Signs* is a lower budget, quiet movie, you don't see much action, or aliens, meaning much of the movie relies on you feeling, and fearing, for the characters.

Graham's backstory plays out over the course of the movie. All we know about him at first is that he used to be a minister, but something happened that robbed him of his belief. Now he's a bitter man void of faith and angry at both God and the man responsible for the car crash that killed Graham's wife (and his trust in God.)

Over the course of the story, Graham must overcome his anger and forgive both the man who caused the accident and God. It's only at the film's climactic moment that he remembers something his wife said — something that not only shows him how to save his family but makes him believe that God was at work and hadn't abandoned him.

You might read something else into that ending. The point is that Graham's redemption and forgiveness of the man he blamed for his wife's death brought him one step closer to being open to forgiving God and believing that He was indeed at work. This allowed him to trust in God that the thing he remembered was of significance to defeating the aliens.

Through healing his inner conflict, Graham managed to overcome his external conflict. And in the end, he is healed and has returned to his job as a minister.

But not every story is as black and white as *Signs*.

Sometimes the good guys lose. Or they win and lose.

A PYRRHIC VICTORY

Sometimes a victory in one area leads to a loss in

another — a pyrrhic victory that costs too damned much.

I won't spoil the best twist in Chan-wook Park's *Oldboy*, but it's an excellent example of a pyrrhic victory.

The South Korean film follows Oh Dae-su, a man who is imprisoned for fifteen years in a cell that looks like a hotel room, by someone he doesn't know for reasons he's not told.

Interestingly, Oh Dae-su starts off as a rather selfish, despicable man. Only during his imprisonment does he become a better person and someone we root for.

After he's released, he sets out to find who imprisoned him and why. And he wants vengeance for the years that he's lost.

That journey is a bloody thrill ride I'm not willing to spoil here.

Oldboy is billed as an action film, and there are a ton of beautifully choreographed scenes (including the infamous hallway fight with a hammer scene that Netflix's *Daredevil* borrowed a few times). But it's the heart of the characters that helps us to feel the impact of what plays out. *Oldboy* manages to be a revenge film where both the hero and the villain are both seeking vengeance. These two paths crash into one of the most memorable, powerful, twisted endings I've ever seen.

No matter whether your hero wins *or* loses or wins *and* loses, he or she should be in a different place than where it all started. And confronting darkness is how you do it.

If you decide on a downer ending, there are still ways to mitigate it so your audience is left satisfied enough to join your next journey.

11

THE DAISY IN THE POST-APOCALYPTIC SIDEWALK

No matter what your characters go through, your story must eventually end. And how you end it might be more important than you think.

Let's imagine your ideal reader. We'll call her Liza.

You know Liza will loooooove the kind of book you've just written. You just need to get that book in her hand. Maybe she finds it on sale. Maybe it's recommended to her by someone else who just read your awesome new book. Maybe someone broke into her house and set it on her nightstand.

That's some next level marketing right there!

The point is, she got your book and you were right; she's loving it.

But she hasn't gotten to the ending yet.

What kind of ending did you deliver?

Is it a tragic ending where you pulled a Dead Baby on Christmas to show how edgy and dark you were?

I get the urge to go full Dead Baby on Christmas. Believe me, I get it. I was killing off main characters long before George R.R. Martin made it cool.

Part of it is the contrarian in me. If you tell me I can't or shouldn't write that sort of ending, I'll probably do it just to prove a point. Or sometimes I'll think, "Wow, nobody's done this before! This'll be really awesome!"

I'm going to close out this chapter with my idea for The Best Movie Ever, which I'm certain nobody's ever done, and it would make me deliriously happy to do it just because it's so out of left field. But I know it would be a mistake.

It's the movie equivalent of a Dead Baby on Christmas.

Sheesh, Dave, how many dead baby jokes are you going to make?

YOU HAVE ISSUES!

Anyway, by the time I'm at the end of writing a book, I'm usually ready to say goodbye to the characters — even the ones I love. Like that annoying family member on Thanksgiving, I don't think too much about killing them off.

But when I reread the book months, or years, later, I'm not there as a writer. I'm a reader instead, experiencing the story on a different level. And I almost always regret my darkest endings.

For two reasons.

First, I've just asked you to spend dozens of hours, or more if it's a series, with these characters. It's rude to kill them all off without some consideration.

Second, there needs to be some hope in the stories I most enjoy. You can destroy the world as we know it in your epic narrative, but you can't end the story with smoking ruins and no sign things will ever be okay again.

There should always be a flower pushing through the cracked sidewalk.

You see, unless this is the last book you plan to write, the end of your story isn't the end of your reader's journey. It is, one hopes, only the beginning.

You want your reader to feel good, or bittersweet, when she reaches the end of your book. The more she enjoys it the more likely she is to buy your next book or dig through your back catalog.

If Liza loves how you ended your book, she's

probably thinking she'll get a similar experience from other books you've written.

But if you left her feeling worse than when she started the story and like all hope is lost, she might think, "Shit, I can get that from turning on the news." Then she's far more likely to go find another author who can make her feel good.

This is one of those rules you should feel free to ignore if you disagree. Some people love dark endings. And they will be more inclined to read all your books if you give them what they want.

Just remember that the dark ending must be earned.

You can't just pull it out of the nowhere like a big, HA! Gotcha! You didn't expect me to kill them all that way, did you?

Speaking of which, back to my idea for The Best Movie Ever.

For a long time, I wanted to be in a position to make any movie I wanted. Usually actors, writers, and directors have to work their way there, starting by making movies the studios believe will make back their investments. It takes a while to get to a point where you can make your big artistic movie.

Here's mine.

.   .   .

IT STARTS off as a romantic comedy. I get the most well-known romantic comedy actor and actress as the lead roles. So when you see the movie poster, you KNOW what kinda movie you're going in to.

Or so you think.

It starts off just like any other rom-com. Girl meets guy, they fall for one another, and it's early going in the movie, long before you typically expect the first obstacle.

Maybe we're in the middle of one of those montages of them having fun at various pretty locales — a park in a rowboat, feeding one another cotton candy at a carnival, ice skating, they're at some cute shop buying souvenirs they can someday show their kids, and whatever else young couples do while falling in love.

In other words, the audience isn't expecting anything.

And then it happens.

They're crossing the street, right in the middle of the montage, and you think they're on their way to whatever next fun thing they're gonna do in the sequence.

But then ... BAM!

They're hit by a giant bus.

Just runs them right the hell over.

An incredibly graphic explosion of flesh and bone and blood all over the street.

Maybe the camera pans over so you see the souvenirs they'll never get to show their kids because their futures were just obliterated in a freak accident.

And the camera just sits there on the carnage. You think it's going to move on to the next scene, but it doesn't.

Instead, it pulls out, but just a bit, so you can see the bus driver get out and weep at what he's done.

Traffic is stopped.

Police and emergency workers show up.

Buzzards are circling the corpses.

And the camera just STAYS on the scene.

You're waiting for something else to happen, but it doesn't.

It's nineteen minutes into the movie, and there's another hour and a half to go of … just this.

And the audience doesn't know what to think.

This CAN'T be a troll right?

There HAS to be a point to this.

The director wouldn't just show an hour and a half of real-time post-accident carnage, would they?

WHO DOES THIS?

The audience is shifting around, wondering if

they should leave, but afraid if they do they'll miss something, like those damned Marvel movie post-credit sequences.

If they wait, there'll be a pay-off.

But nothing happens.

The camera just continues rolling.

And the movie doesn't go on for another hour and a half, but three more hours!

A Director's Cut.

WHO the hell does this?

I would.

That's who.

And then, as word got out about the movie, people would wonder why I did it. Years later, there would be college film students writing papers on the movie, arguing whether it was some artistic statement on the fickleness of fate or man's search for meaning through tacky souvenirs.

WHAT DID DAVE MEAN? WHAT WAS THE POINT?

And it would be the most awesome movie ever. And, in my dreams of making this movie, I'm there on opening night, disguised, sitting in the back, enjoying the confused, stunned reaction, laughing inside.

But — and here's the point of all of this — as

clever as I'd feel in making such a messed-up joke of a movie, nobody would ever watch another movie I made, and rightfully so.

I'd become known as that director, the one who trolled his audience. Nobody would ever take a chance on me again.

People would be afraid they'd have a repeat performance of me dashing their expectations. And those who did like my avant-garde movie would be disappointed in any attempt to make a more commercial film.

Anyway, the point of that, other than to impress you with my idea for the Best Movie Ever, is to reiterate that endings matter. How the audience feels about the story is how they're going to feel about you as a creator.

One thing I should mention is that everybody I've told that story to has gotten the joke. They laughed at the idea. They saw what I was trying to do. They probably think I'm crazy, but they still got the joke.

But this weekend I told my wife the idea for the movie over lunch.

She doesn't share my love for dark stories or dark humor. She's the kind of person who would go see the rom-com movie I was pretending to make.

My explaining how this movie would be a rom-com maybe raised her hopes that I was finally going to write something that didn't take a decidedly left turn into Doom and Gloom Town.

After I got to the reveal, she just stared at me.

Horrified.

Which is exactly the kind of reaction I was hoping for. I sat there laughing while she questioned the life choices that had led her to that moment.

It's not quite the same as sitting there on opening night with an audience, but it'll be as close as I'll probably get to that dream.

12

CREATING VILLAINS WITH DEPTH

WHAT DOES YOUR VILLAIN WANT?

Back in the day, Hollywood did a shitty job of creating realistic villains. Whether it was the man who wanted to destroy the world because of ... reasons, or the masked killer who wanted to kill teenagers having sex at summer camp for ... reasons, villains really sucked.

In real life, villains aren't one-note monsters — except in Florida. Villains in Florida do it for the memes. But most other evil people have other interests or a softer side.

Hitler liked puppies, stamp collecting, and long walks on the beach.

Okay, I totally made that up, but you get the idea. People are multi-faceted, even your bad guys and gals. They have inner desires and conflicts just like the rest of us.

Consider one of my favorite bad guys in television, *Breaking Bad's* Walter White.

I won't spoil anything other than the arc of the show's main character, which you can get from the premise of "turning Mr. Chips into Scarface."

Walter White is the perfect example of a nuanced character who starts out as a hero and whose reasons for slowly becoming a villain are easy to understand. He starts off in the show as a put-upon milquetoast teacher who finds out he has cancer. We're with him as he suffers the indignities of life and his brother-in-law (the alpha male DEA agent, Hank) emasculates him jokingly in front of his family — on Walter's birthday, no less.

The guy could not be a more sympathetic figure at the show's start. He's the hero being squeezed into a situation where the only way he sees to provide money for his family is to become a meth dealer.

Because of his cunning and intellect, he's damned resourceful at his job, quickly rising up the food chain in the drug underworld.

His motives for embarking on his criminal enterprise start off as noble, a reason that we can understand — to leave money for his family. It's his external need. And an excellent motivation that feels real and is easy to believe.

But, eventually, another reason is exposed — Walt's internal need to reclaim his lost manhood, to get some power. This is what drives him to become the bad guy as the series continues.

Walter White is the primary protagonist during much of the series, but he's also its antagonist near the end, with some of the focus shifting toward his protege, Jesse Pinkman.

Breaking Bad defies the usual set-up so viewers are torn as to whether they want Walter to succeed at the end and serves as an A+ example of villains done correctly.

Even the show's other antagonist, the ice-cold kingpin and very professional Gus Fring, isn't a one-note character. Not only does he serve as Walter and Jesse's nemesis, but he has his own character arc and fall from grace. Experience his backstory and it's hard not to feel some sympathy for him. Maybe even root for him a bit.

Sometimes the biggest difference between whether a character is the protagonist or antagonist is simply our viewpoint. And where your heroes benefit from being well-rounded and having a dark side, your villains can also reap the rewards of having another side to them.

You want your villains to feel real. You want their goals and motivations to make sense, if not to the reader, at least to the characters themselves.

You might be writing a dark fantasy story where the villain is trying to kill all elves, creating an elf genocide.

And that's an allegorical premise ripe for story ideas.

But why is your villain doing this?

Perhaps our villain's people were oppressed by elves at a time when the roles were reversed and the elves were in power. Maybe there's something personal in all of this. Could be a combination of things.

Our villain now has a motive to kill all the elves. It might not be a good one, a reason you would kill all the elves, but as long as it's good enough for him to want to, your reader will understand how he wound up this way.

It's all too easy to imagine villains will see the error of their ways when they're doing all their evil shit. But a belief that they are doing good already is terrifying because if they believe their mission is righteous, then their behavior can be reprehensible.

So, what should the villain want?

In most cases, either the hero and villain want the same thing but both can't have it or they are seeking diametrically opposing outcomes.

In the first instance, they both might be seeking some powerful artifact. They might have different reasons for wanting it. Maybe the bad guy wants it so he can take over the realm and the good guy wants it to save the kingdom. Kind of how both Jack and Rachel wanted custody of Rob. They want the same thing for different reasons.

In the second instance, we'll return to our elf genocide story.

Our hero wants to free the elven slaves, to create an elf state where they can live free. Perhaps they even want to depose the bad guy. The bad guy wants to continue to eradicate all the elves until the threat, as he sees them, is gone.

Both wants should be integral to their character.

One of my favorite episodes of AMC's *The Walking Dead* was when they revealed the Governor's backstory. You learned how normal he'd been. Despite the evil shit he did, he felt it was absolutely necessary for the greater good to protect his people.

Fiction is filled with fantastic villains — characters who were once weak and powerless to help those around them. They then react by overcompen-sating, viewing any kindness as a frailty that could cost them the throne or their people's lives.

Whenever I talk about *The Walking Dead*, I usually tell people my idea for the show. Something that would've been pretty amazing if they'd done it.

Around the time AMC realized they had a hit with *The Walking Dead*, they should've started a spinoff series. Not *Fear the Walking Dead*, but a show that had the Governor as the lead, as the hero, long before he appeared on the main series.

You get the audience invested in him and what he's doing. They see him as the hero!

And then ... slowly the two shows would cross over until the audience was watching an all-out war between people that fans of both shows would've seen as "the good guys."

That would've been an amazing thing.

We're doing something like that with one of our future stories.

ADDITIONAL DEPTH

So, we've got the main conflict and we under-stand why our villain is doing whatever they're doing.

Now what?

Now you want to add some additional depth. Since nobody is all bad, this is a great place to dive into the things your villain does when not engaged in his dastardly deeds.

Maybe your villain has an interesting hobby or a side you don't normally associate with their type, like Hannibal Lecter being a gourmand. He could be really into comic books like *Unbreakable's* Mr. Glass. Or your villain is into Disney and even painted some cartoon characters, as Hitler is said to have done.

That one I'm not making up!

Perhaps your stone cold killer has a soft, vulnerable side brought out by his shrink, like Tony in HBO's *The Sopranos.*

Don't be afraid to give your villain some depth, especially if it provides additional context to their life and why they do what they do. But even if unrelated to the main story arc or their evil deeds, quirky or unusual hobbies can provide levity or humor to balance the story.

This also makes your characters feel like living, breathing entities that existed long before your reader ever met them. That's the kind of stuff I dig in a story, feeling like the characters, and the world, are real enough to draw breath on their own.

13

SYMPATHY FOR THE DEVIL

SOMETIMES, despite the fact that the villain is vile and has hurt, or killed, characters you like, you can't help but like them.

Take Negan from *The Walking Dead*.

Negan's introduction was him killing one of the most beloved characters on the show in a very brutal fashion.

Yet, within a couple of seasons, fans of the show have come to love him. Or at least hate him a little less.

Why is that? How do you go from bashing someone's head in with a barbed-wire baseball bat to becoming a charming anti-hero whose redemption you're rooting for?

Part of it is just that ... Negan is a charming

asshole who says what a lot of people are thinking. He, like our own Boricio Wolfe, is all id — a mix of walking bravado and hilarious one-liners. He screws with you mentally before hurting you physically.

He does what he wants, when he wants, and without giving a damn what anybody thinks. A lot of people wish they could get away with the things Negan does or says, but they can't because, generally, society is polite.

Also, while Negan seems like a monster when you first meet him, he's not. He doesn't just kill for shits and giggles. He's not some asshole hunting innocents for sport. He's doing what he thinks he must to protect his people.

He doesn't see Rick and his crew as the good people that viewers do. He sees them as pains in the asses who have been screwing with his crew and are posing a threat. He must take action or risk losing his post-apocalyptic kingdom to interlopers.

Negan strikes, viciously enough that everyone will remember and think twice about crossing him again. Then he shows mercy in letting the group go free, so long as they abide by his rules. Yeah, the rules suck. And Rick's group hates him and what he did, but viewers eventually understand his side.

While Negan's methods are awful, they're not

arbitrary. They serve a purpose, and the character is doing what he believes to be the right thing. Sometimes leaders see the right thing as a difficult thing that only they can do. Almost as if it's their burden and only they have the guts to do the difficult things that must be done to preserve order.

Whether you subscribe to this theory of post-apocalyptic law and order is besides the point. Negan's logic is consistent with his character.

He's someone people can look up to. He keeps his people safe. He enforces laws, strictly. In the post-apocalyptic world of *The Walking Dead*, one can easily argue that you need people like Negan to keep the even scarier people from kicking down your door.

People also like Negan because he's charming and funny. Humor goes a long way in such a bleak, unforgiving show. It's a release valve for the constantly rising tension. The audience appreciates the moments of humor and the frequent vulgarities that come out of this character's mouth.

The Walking Dead also gave Negan a softer side in the show as he developed a friendship with Rick's daughter, Judith Grimes. He's still an asshole, but you also see his softer side and his protectiveness of the child.

No matter how much you hate him for killing (NAME REDACTED just in case you haven't seen the show), you can't help but think, "Awww, he's a big softie," after seeing him interact with Judith.

Giving your villains a softer side doesn't just make them more relatable.

It can also make them ... scarier.

Let's say you write your own version of a villainous leader like Negan, a character doing his best to survive in a zombie post-apocalyptic world. (Obviously, he's not Negan Two; you're gonna create an original bad guy. But he's enough like him to serve this example.) Negan Two has created this safe place where his henchmen plunder other villages to get supplies for his people. He's the bad guy to your version of Rick, but to his people, he's their savior. The one guy keeping them safe. So of course, they are loyal and grateful.

Now, imagine if you gave him a daughter.

Think how much scarier he would be if he wasn't just fighting to keep his kingdom and people safe, but he was battling for the safety of his child. Because remember, he doesn't know your version of Rick is a good guy. He sees only that this guy and his crew are killing his people. How far will Negan Two go if he doesn't stop them?

His motivations would be that much deeper. Negan Two would fight your hero even harder. He could not stand the idea of losing because that could mean his child's death. Maybe even, ironically, via baseball bat.

What would you do to save your kids from that fate?

Now imagine what someone like Negan would do.

That's way scarier than a bad guy waving a bat around.

KIDS MAKE GREAT WEAKNESSES

Another villain, though I think of him more as an anti-hero, is Mike Ehrmantraut of *Breaking Bad* and *Better Call Saul.*

He's an old codger who acts just like you'd expect the moment you see him — takes no shit and will never spare feelings. He's a tough, no-nonsense, former Philadelphia cop who later becomes head of security, cleaner, and a hit-man. Mike is a threat to our heroes, Walt and Jesse, but viewers can't help but feel for the guy, especially when they see how far he's going to redeem himself with his dead son's wife and his granddaughter, Kaylee. Everything he does is for them.

And, as we learn more of his backstory, especially in the stellar *Better Call Saul* Season One, Episode Six, "Five-O," we see just how ordinary and sad Mike really is. How far his choices, and his circumstances, have pushed him. We can easily imagine being in his shoes. The episode is heartbreaking and unforgettable.

While Mike isn't necessarily the "bad guy" in these shows which traffic almost exclusively gray areas, he still serves as a great example on how to give a tough, menacing character a sympathetic side. It makes them more well-rounded and, as we discussed earlier, even scarier.

14

BUT NOT TOO MUCH SYMPATHY

So, you've made your well-rounded bad guy. Hell, we might even like this guy now. But before you start swiping right on Tinder to hook up with this dude, remember — he's still a bad guy.

Your audience should be properly scared. And maybe unsettled. We need reminders of just how unhinged your villain can become. We need to see what a threat he is to the other characters in your story.

Again, I'll turn to the master of complex characters, Vince Gilligan, the creator, head writer, executive producer, and showrunner of *Breaking Bad*. It's almost as if he thought it was a personal challenge to see how far he could take his protagonist-turned-antagonist, Walter White, and have viewers still like Walt.

Gilligan has said he wanted viewers to hate Walter.

In asking how far the audience would go along with Walt before they finally stopped rooting for him, he made them almost complicit in the character's crimes. I can't help but think part of that was to show the moral grays that exist in society ... how a beloved family man can also be this monstrous drug lord.

He slowly peeled away Walt's humanity in layers until we saw just how far he would go. At some point in the show's run, Walt could've walked away from the role. But he didn't. And we saw that he was no longer in the game to provide for his family; by then it was only for the power.

I do need to spoil a few things about the show to continue this discussion. Just to illustrate how far Gilligan took Walter White.

SPOILERS FOR BREAKING BAD BELOW

.   .   .

THE FIRST TIME most of us realized just how much of a monster Walter White truly was occurred when he walked in on his partner, Jesse, sleeping with his girlfriend, Jane. She was passed out and choking from a heroin overdose. Walter could've intervened and saved her. But, because he viewed her as a threat to his working relationship with Jesse, he just stood there and allowed her to die then slowly sneaked away, leaving a clueless Jesse to wake up to his girlfriend's dead body.

Jesse was devastated, and so were we.

The next most heinous thing Walt did was poison Jesse's next girlfriend's young son. He was trying to erode Jesse's trust in Gus Fring and poisoned the kid so Jesse would think Gus had done it to send a message. The child didn't die, but he could have. His fate is irrelevant, though. The takeaway is that Walt saw the child as expendable.

The third time Vince reminded us of what a monster Walt had become was when he killed Mike Ehrmantraut, one of my favorite characters in the *Breaking Bad* or any universe. That was the moment that pushed me off of Team Walt. Vince had finally convinced me the man had to pay.

END OF SPOILERS

. . .

BECAUSE WE WENT THROUGH SO much effort to make your villain a well-rounded, maybe even sometimes sympathetic character, every now and then you should shake things up and remind people of just how bad they are.

Your bad guy is not someone to take lightly.

He is a threat to your hero and can flip the eff out at any moment!

15

FINDING INSPIRATION FOR YOUR DARK CHARACTERS

WHETHER IT'S your hero or your villain, there's no shortage of inspirations out there for flawed, dark characters.

For villains, look no further than any of the sociopathic but charismatic real-life villains. Whether it be the charming serial killer or the alluring, ruthless politician or the attractive yet callous celebrity, there's no shortage of assholes and fuck-ups to inspire you.

I don't like to write about real people, but I do think studying these people and how they tick can help you create an amalgamation of the worst of the worst. Then you add some touches of good qualities — unless you're writing a Florida Man character — and you've got yourself a villain.

There are also any number of flawed heroes out there to serve as an excellent start on yours.

We've all seen the politician who meant well but was undone by greed or a sex scandal. Or, as is probably more often the case, he or she started off with the best of intentions but was co-opted by tough decisions and unholy alliances. Soon enough, favors were owed to people who had bad intentions.

We've also seen cops who crossed the line or succumbed to vices that put their jobs in jeopardy either out of frustration or in attempt to do what they thought to be the right thing.

No matter the walk of life, there is someone out there who has admirable qualities that might have even been a hero to others but screwed up in some major way.

Nobody is all good or all bad.

Except Florida Man. Stay away from that guy!

Find real-life examples of heroes and villains. Read biographies of famous people. Get a feel for the things that not only weaken our heroes, but make them succumb to their flaws.

Then give them a redemption storyline.

Everybody loves a good redemption story.

Obviously we're not going to try and redeem the worst offenders. I don't see anyone lining up to turn

Bill Cosby or Roman Polanski into sympathetic heroes anytime soon. But there are many weaknesses we can forgive — especially the ones we, ourselves, could've easily fallen into.

It's not difficult to imagine our own lives if things had gone the wrong way.

Maybe this alternate version of you got addicted to painkillers after a bout with back pain or surgery. Or they lost everything in the housing crash and turned to a life of crime out of desperation to provide for their family. Turned to unhealthy vices to deal with a past trauma.

It's easy to judge others for giving in to their vices or finding themselves on the wrong side of the law. But a writer needs to think beyond that and try to put themselves in that person's shoes.

It's our job as writers to imagine other people's lives. And in order to do our jobs well, we must understand other people's lives. That also means we need to see things not in black and white, but in shades of gray. And, perhaps, even have some sympathy for those society typically turns its back on.

When we see people in their totality, with lives, needs, wishes, and mistakes, we're better able to write more believable characters. Capable of exploring the darkness in a more thorough way.

PLAYING PRETEND

Remember how I used to pretend my Star Wars action figures were actually super heroes? Well, you can do that, too.

And I'm not talking about toys, unless that's your thing, or your kids have awesome toys they ignore.

No, I'm talking about using fictional characters on TV and movies as a character development exercise. Kind of like fan-fiction, except you aren't going to be publishing this. It's just for practice.

I haven't done fan-fiction since I was a kid, but I haven't got anything against the genre. Hell, if *Twilight* fan-fiction can inspire a hit like *Fifty Shades of Grey*, then we ought not to look too dismissively at the form.

Take any show you watch and find a few characters who aren't the lead. The more obscure or background the characters, the better. Choose one, say the male lead's younger sister.

What do you know about her?

Create a new backstory for her. Make her the star of the show.

How would the show change?

What darkness does your character deal with? What does she have to overcome? Maybe seeing the show through her eyes puts her at odds with the main character, turning him into the antagonist.

Or take a hero and villain on a show and swap their roles. Find a way to make viewers or readers despise the hero and have sympathy for the villain.

You can also do this with real-life people. Try and imagine their lives and how they got to where they are. I do this all the time while out in public. I love people watching. Nine times out of ten, I'm imagining their lives.

Do this in a non-judgmental manner to better tell a story from that person's point-of-view. Maybe you choose to focus on the middle-aged man on the bench holding his wife's purse.

What is his darkness?

What is his origin story?

How can he get past that darkness?

What stands in his way?

How do you see his story playing out?

The more you do these kinds of exercises, getting out of your head and into the minds of different types of people, the better characters you're likely to write, and the more equipped you'll be to dip in and out of the darkness.

READY TO GO INTO THE DARKNESS?

When I think back to Younger Dave, sitting in the back of class, friendless and scribbling stories in his notebook, I wish I could've told him things would be okay, he was on the right path, and he shouldn't let fear hold him back for so long.

Maybe I'll write about that fear more in my next non-fiction title.

But then I think about how much the darkness has helped to shape me into the writer I am.

We are the sum of our experiences. And it's all too easy to wallow in them and to think about the things that didn't go right. Or to hate the injustice of Fate.

But none of those things helps us move forward. They're a surrender. They're letting darkness win. They're abdicating the very agency we want in our characters.

They're giving up.

And we can never give up.

Writing about darkness has allowed me to see things I might not have seen otherwise.

It would've been all too easy to blame my bullies for many of my fears and anxieties. It would've been easy to hold on to the hate I felt. But what good does that do me longterm?

Holding on to the hate, for me, would've allowed fear to continue to have its way with me. I would've been angry at a memory of a person, or, in some cases, a ghost.

And to what point?

Far better to try and see the events in my life and the people who hurt me through a different filter. Far better to try and see things from a zoomed out view, where I can realize the bullying was never about me. Where I could see not just the bad shit that happened, but also the bad things that could've happened but didn't.

When you can explore your darkness through writing, you can exert a control over it.

Remember that guy, Tony? The friendly fifth grader that hit me in the balls with a dumbbell?

Well, I was terrified of him for years. And I always saw him as that evil kid who hit me in the balls then called my mom a fat bitch. And it would've been easy to always see him that way. I hated him as much as I feared him.

One day, either late in high school or just after

high school, I got stuck somewhere and had to walk home many miles.

Tony drove by in his sports car, and I felt this gnawing in the pit of my gut — that old hate and fear.

He slowed down, turned around, then pulled his car alongside me.

We hadn't run into each other much over the years. Despite him being my first bully, he'd quickly moved on after middle school. But as he pulled up next to me, I wondered why.

And I was afraid.

He looked at me and asked, "Need a ride?"

I was shocked. And a part of me thought he was just looking to take advantage of my naive self again. That I'd get in his car and he'd take me to the woods and beat the hell out of me or something. Who knew what he was capable of? I remembered that look of glee as he hit me with the dumbbells.

Pure evil.

I had a long walk ahead of me, though. And it's Florida Hot. If you're lucky enough not to be familiar with Florida's particular brand of hot, being outside in the summer is like being in a sauna, minus the naked people you might encounter in a sauna. So I had a real dilemma. Do I trust him again? If he did something this time, at least I wouldn't be caught off guard. I'm pretty sure I palmed a pen I could use as a weapon if needed as I got into his car.

And he drove me home.

We made awkward small talk, and I can't remember what either of us said, but I realized in that moment that he was no longer the person I thought him to be. Maybe he'd never been just that person. Yeah, he was an asshole who did something horrible, but he had apparently changed.

Tony didn't have to give me a ride home.

But I think a part of him was trying to make amends.

And it was the first time I realized my bullies weren't all the monsters I'd made them out to be. Some of them had grown up and become responsible. Maybe even nice. Sure, some probably went on to be wife-beating assholes, but still, my hate would be wasted on them.

As I said before, villains are never the villains in their stories.

People I hated, people I absolutely made into monstrosities in my mind, capable of God Only Knows What, are merely human. Like me ... just a bit more asshole than me.

They're not these all-powerful deities who have dominion over my life.

Unless I give them that strength.

Writing has helped me channel some of that fear, hate, and helplessness I felt. It's helped me find a place to put some of the residual pain I'm still working through. And it's helped me see outside myself, which has helped me connect to others I might not otherwise have connected with.

I've heard from many readers who have told me their stories, many even worse than my own. And they've told me how our writing has helped them get through some shit.

I think back to that younger version of me who had hoped to someday touch people's lives and provide escape. And now I'm doing it for a living!

So, now I ask you — what is your darkness?

How can you explore it in a meaningful way for not only yourself but for your readers?

Think about the things you've struggled with. The things you've watched your friends or loved ones struggle through. You're not alone. They're not alone. There's a lot of us out there struggling with dark things.

It's your job now to write about them.

No matter what things you've been through in

your life, you have something valuable to contribute to others.

So long as we can write, we can create our own story and design our own escape. Perhaps we can even help show others that escape is possible.

And darkness isn't eternal.

ACCESS THE VAULT

The best way to retain what you just learned is through reminders and application.

We've created a **60-Second Summary** of the key points in this book for you to print and keep handy as you begin to incorporate what you learned.

You'll find the summary, PLUS *all our extra downloadables for the entire Stone Tablet range* in our Extras Vault.

Visit **SterlingAndStone.net/Extras** to get access.

Made in the USA
Coppell, TX
20 October 2019